OLMSTED'S VISION:
THE LANDSCAPE OF FLORHAM

Walter Cummins
Linda Snyder
Arthur T. Vanderbilt II
Edward Zimmermann

Florham Books

Olmsted's Vision: The Landscape of Florham

Prepared by Walter Cummins, Linda Snyder, Arthur T. Vanderbilt II, and Edward Zimmermann

Copyright © 2018

ISBN: 978-0-692-10196-4

Published by Florham Books

First Florham Books Edition 2018

Photographs and Images

The cover photograph is by Mark Hillringhouse. The majority of the interior photographs are by Linda Snyder. Others are by Mark Hillringhouse, Shirley Burden, Johnston Stewart, and from the Fairleigh Dickinson University digital archieves. Topographical surveys and planting plans are from the Olmsted Archives, Brookline, Massachusetts.

With great thanks to Peter Woolley,
Florham Campus Provost, 2012-2017,
for his commitment to awareness
of Florham's history and for
his efforts to maintain and
enhance the beauty of its landscape

OLMSTED'S VISION

If it hadn't been for Frederick Law Olmsted, Florham never would have existed. His vision saw the potential that lay in the acreage when it was nothing more than rough, overgrown ground, partially a swamp that needed drainage. That ability to imagine the future of a landscape lay at the heart of his genius. And he convinced Hamilton Twombly to finance the transformation of the site into his country estate.

Olmsted could not draw beyond rough sketches. He was not a horticulturalist in the sense of extensive knowledge of trees and plants. His gift was holistic, conceiving of the shapes, designs, and colors of an area in a manner that changed the future of American landscape architecture in the late nineteenth and early twentieth centuries. From coast to coast, from north to south, we still may witness the wonders of his genius, whether they are the products of his vision, or of his descendants, or of the many he influenced.

Olmsted also possessed an exceptional ability for organization and delegation. He hired people expert in the details of fulfilling his desires by developing detailed plans and finding the trees and foliage that would realize the shapes, sizes, and colors he had seen in his mind.

In the century and a quarter that has passed since Olmsted envisioned Florham, a great deal has changed. In fact, Olmsted had retired before Florham was completed. How much of the estate was specifically "his" remains in question. And over time, age and storms have uprooted original trees, new trees and gardens came into existence, new buildings have been constructed. But, underlying any and all of these changes, at the heart of Florham's existence as an estate and as a campus, we still may see the vision of Frederick Law Olmsted.

CONTENTS

Aerial view of Florham as an estate

Aerial view of Florham as a campus

PREFACE

As significant as the mansion of a great Gilded Age estate like Florham—the New Jersey country home of Florence Vanderbilt Twombly—was its landscape. This book explores how that greatest of all landscape architects—Frederick Law Olmsted—visualized 1,200 acres of woodlands and scrub growth and swamps and transformed them into a magical country retreat for a family which could afford, and demanded, "the best of the best."

Today, over a century after Olmsted laid out his vision, and boatloads of Italian immigrant workers labored with picks and shovels and wheelbarrows to realize that vision, you can still feel Olmsted's magic.

Enter the Florham campus of Fairleigh Dickinson University--which purchased the Twombly estate in 1958—through the formal entrance off Madison Avenue, through the open iron gates set on two massive brick pillars flanked by a weeping European beech, follow the road past the Gatehouse and under an allee of American linden. Southern Japanese hemlock, Western hemlock, Washington English yew, and a grove of Japanese false cypress grace the dramatic approach to the Mansion. Adorning the great lawn in front of the Mansion are two large specimens of Cedar of Lebanon, a large Nordmann fir and weeping Canadian hemlock, and a spectacular linden. And as you wander through this park-like setting, you will encounter a collection of common boxwood greater than fifteen feet in in height and width and stands of oaks that were there prior to the development of the estate and which are visible on an 1890 topographic site survey.

Throughout Mrs. Twombly's reign at Florham, the landscaping was even more elaborate. In a black and white home movie taken in the early 1930's by her fabled French chef, Joseph Donon, you can see the lush plantings of azalea and rhododendrons that lined the carefully raked gravel drive from the Madison Avenue entrance to the Mansion, masses of Spring bulbs in bloom, elaborate rose gardens and everywhere, flowering shrubs.

Much of this splendor has of course made way for University needs. But the wonder of Olmsted's work, and the work of subsequent landscapers recognized in this book, is still evident everywhere--in the perfect siting of the Mansion which suddenly arises, dreamlike, before you as you make your way down the drive, in the siting of the Orangerie and the Carriage House, in the ancient specimen trees, in the beautiful Italian Garden and in the Fountain gardens behind the Mansion.

As Ruth Twombly wrote of her father, Hamilton Twombly: "He decided to put a great deal of his energy and his love of the beautiful into creating an earthly paradise for his four children." And a paradise it was, and is still today. In this landscape, Olmsted created a lasting work of art as much as a Rembrandt or Michelangelo.

This is the third in our series of books about Florham.

The first was *Florham: An American Treasure: From the Gilded Age Vanderbilt-Twombly Estate to a Contemporary University Campus* (2016), which focuses on the history of what is still today the eighth largest home ever built in the United States, its decades as a "Downton Abbey" style residence, and then, for the past sixty years, its transformation into a modern university campus.

The second book of this series about Florham is titled *"The Richest and Most Famous Private Chef in the World"—Joseph Donon: Gilded Age Dining at Florham with Florence Vanderbilt Twombly* (2017). This book deals with the heart of a great estate: dinner parties. And for the first time, it publishes the memoirs of Chef Donon, Mrs. Twombly's beloved chef for almost four decades. His reminisces provide perhaps the most complete "downstairs" look at a Gilded Age estate.

And now, with this, our third book: a trilogy of love poems to Florham. The perfect place to end? Or a place to begin? For the more we learn about Florham and the way life was lived on a Gilded Age estate, the more discoveries we've made and the more tantalizing mysteries remain for us, or others, to solve and reveal.

Walter Cummins
Linda Snyder
Arthur T. Vanderbilt II
Edward Zimmermann

Approaching the Mansion in the 1930s Donon film

Approaching the Mansion today

OLMSTED AND FLORHAM

Florham owes its existence, first as a country estate and today as a university campus, to the extraordinary vision of Fredrick Law Olmsted, who conceived of the possibilities inherent within those hundreds of acres and convinced the property owners, Florence Vanderbilt and Hamilton Twombly, to support its creation.

Frederick Law Olmsted, Sr. (April 26, 1822–August 28, 1903), in addition to being recognized as one of the founders of American landscape architecture, was also recognized as a journalist, social critic, and public administrator. Among the many municipal parks he designed in cities throughout the United States, with his senior partner Calvert Vaux, were New York's Central Park and Brooklyn's Prospect Park. Olmsted also designed master plans for several universities including Stanford University, the University of California at Berkeley, Trinity College in Hartford, and Johns Hopkins University in Baltimore.

The landscape design of Florham was one of Olmsted's final projects, and he had retired in 1895, disabled by Alzheimer's, before the estate opened in 1897. Still, Florham can be considered an Olmsted creation. He conceived of the property and developed the plan followed by the Olmsted firm after it passed on to his son, Frederick, Jr., and his stepson, John Charles. William S. Manning, landscape architect for the Olmsted firm, probably played a major role in the final implementation of Olmsted's vision for Florham. Several other landscape architects were involved in various phases. In the years after Florham opened, additional gardens were created to blend with the initial plan.

Yet, even today, more than a century later, visitors to the estate—now the university campus—will see that it embodies all the characteristics of an Olmsted site, design elements that made him the most famous and sought-after landscape architect of his time, and one who continues to be a standard for all who succeeded him in seeking "the genius of a place." His success at Florham makes it another primary Olmsted achievement.

Writing of Florham after attending the 1955 auction after the deaths of Florence Vanderbilt Twombly and her daughter Ruth that marked the end of the Twombly era, Brendan Gill, *The New Yorker's* famed writer, captured what the 13,000 visitors saw: "Florham," he wrote, "is everything one thinks an English country seat should be, with the greenest of green lawns running on into groves of oak and beech, and, rising against the sky at the end of a long graveled drive, a hundred-room house of rosy brick, its roof bristling with chimneys, its many doors open to the summer air." He noted "the dainty palace of an orangerie, all arched windows and glint of glass … the charming crisscross of gardens and paved walks, of pavilions, pergolas, urns on pedestals and grave Greek statues."

Fortunately, more than sixty years after that auction day, with Florham a thriving university campus, Gill's description still applies. The "vision" that Olmsted revealed in his initial plans for the estate lives on for all who walk its paths.

Olmsted's Accomplishments

Even his best-known accomplishments as a landscape architect suggest a man of impressive resolve and resourcefulness: co-designer of Central Park, the first great American urban park; head of the first Yosemite commission; leader of the campaign to protect Niagara Falls; designer of the Capitol Grounds and West Front terrace; site planner for the Great White City of the 1893 World's Columbian Exposition; planner of Boston's "Emerald Necklace" of green space and of park systems in many other cities.

With his Central Park partner, Calvert Vaux, Olmsted coined the term "landscape architect," and with Vaux, he invented the concept of the "parkway"—a landscape drive for pleasure vehicles separate from commercial carts and wagons—with an 1868 design in Brooklyn. Olmsted himself defined what the large urban park in America would be and created the first park systems and urban greenways in this country. He play an instrumental role in the United States' first experiment in scientific forestry at George Washington Vanderbilt's Biltmore estate near Ashville, North Carolina.

Olmsted designed more parks and public recreation grounds than any landscape designer before him, and carried out more commissions that any predecessor in his art. In doing so, he established the importance of the landscape architect in the planning of parks, parkways, park systems, scenic reservations, residential communities, academic institutions, and private estates. His style of landscape design still exerts a strong influence on his profession and has transformed the public and private life of the people of the United States.

Central Park

Olmsted's Goals
in His Own Words

"... the highest value of a park must be expected to lie in elements and qualities of scenery to which the mind of those benefiting by them is liable, at the time the benefit is received, to give little conscious cogitation, and which, though not at all beyond study, are of too complex, subtle and spiritual a nature to be readily checked off, item by item, like a jeweler's or a florist's wares."

"A park is a work of art, designed to produce certain effects upon the mind of men. There should be nothing in it, absolutely nothing—not a foot of surface nor a spear of grass—which does not represent study, design, a sagacious consideraton & application of known laws of cause & effect with reference to that end."

Olmsted's Ten Design Principles

1. Respect "the genius of a place"
2. Subordinate details to the whole
3. The art is to conceal art
4. Aim for the unconscious
5. Avoid fashion for fashion's sake
6. Formal training isn't required
7. Words matter
8. Stand for something
9. Utility trumps ornament
10. Never too much, hardly enough

The heart of these principles may be found in his belief that his goal was to reveal the inherent qualities of the place rather than to impose an external design upon it.

Olmsted's vision for a piece of land parallels that of Michelangelo about sculpture: "Every block of stone has a statue inside it and it is the task of the sculptor to discover it."

For Olmsted, such revelation did not mean passivity; that is, just cosmetically enhancing what already existed. For him "the genius of a place" had to be fashioned. He added contours and shapes, planted trees and shrubbery, imagined vistas to bring out the essence of what lay within.

Olmsted clarifies the role of the landscape architect in a 1875 letter to Dr. Henry F. Hill: "That is precisely what landscape gardening should do I think, make improvements by design which nature might by chance."

This was the Gilded Age, a time of magnificent homes that were architectural masterpieces and estates with wide vistas, emulations of the finest properties of the British aristocracy. Before Florham, Olmsted already had played a central role in other Vanderbilt family country homes. At the time of Florham's creation, he was engrossed in the making of Biltmore, the 120,000-acre estate in Asheville, NC, that became the home of Florence's youngest brother, George Washington Vanderbilt. The house was then and still is the largest private home in America, with its more than two hundred rooms.

Biltmore garden

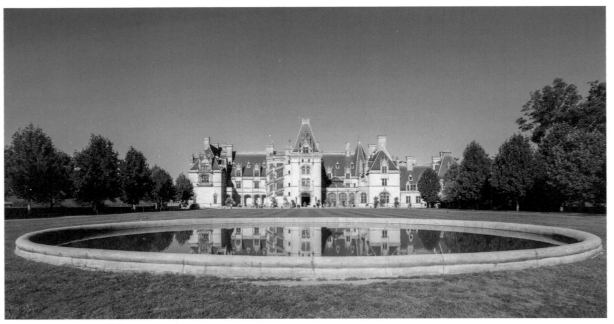

Biltmore Estate

Olmsted and Hamilton Twombly

Florham would never have come into existence without Frederick Law Olmsted and his ability to convince Hamilton Twombly to create a great estate, a country house domain equal to Twombly's stature.

Twombly and his wife, Florence Vanderbilt Twombly, joined a number of other millionaires in Morris County, New Jersey, in the final years of the nineteenth century. In addition to the company of social peers, the area offered space and greenery as well as a train line to New York City and offices in the financial district.

In 1887, the Twomblys rented and later purchased a large home built in 1872-73 by Charles Danforth, a successful inventor and manufacturer of railway engines who died in 1875, soon after his home was completed. The Twomblys originally planned to expand the Danforth home, and develop the landscape, for which they hired Frederick Law Olmsted in 1889. The Olmsted firm designed the landscape for the country homes of several of Florence Twombly's siblings, most famously her brother George at Biltmore, but also her sister Emily at Elm Court in Lenox, Massachusetts, her sister Eliza at Shelburne Farm in Shelburne, Vermont, her brother Frederick at Rough Point in Newport, Rhode Island, as well as the Vanderbilt Mausoleum on Staten Island.

21

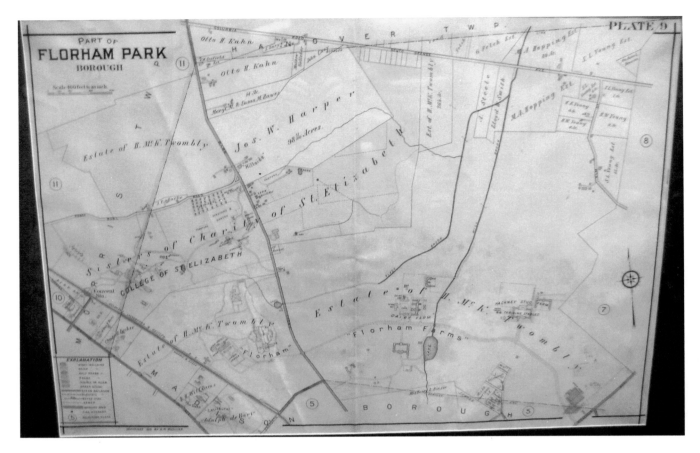

As a source of food and provisions for their life in the Danforth home, Twombly began acquiring nearby land, an expanse of property that would eventually become Florham. To accumulate the land, Hamilton Twombly made 37 separate purchases, beginning with the Danforth Farm and the Miller Tract where the Saddle Stables were located. Later, a parcel to the north was obtained in an exchange with St. Elizabeth's, the Sisters of Charity. In total, the property came to 1,200 acres.

Olmsted told Twombly his plan for the Danforth property was not sufficiently impressive, the house too small, the property too limited. He argued that the result would have been "interesting," though not "grand." And so, he convinced Twombly to build a totally new estate on the land he had acquired as a farm to provide for "the Danforth Place." Instead, Omlsted urged Twombly to build "a large house on the hill on the other side of the railroad," that is, the line that went through Twombly's land holdings.

Hamilton Twombly's Acquisition of the Land for Florham

Although he did not know he would be building a great estate when he accumulated the acreage that became Florham, Hamilton Twombly began his quest to purchase a large area of land in 1890, first planning to create a farm to supply his first Morris County home. Robert J. Nish, Kathleen W. Nish, and W. Cary Edwards, Jr. documented the stages of his acquisitions through a land title search, in conjunction with the American Civilization Institute of Morristown, New Jersey, in 1968. Their report may be found in the Fairleigh Dickinson University archives.

The report's authors explained their procedures: "The major portion of our working hours was spent in the Record Room of the Morris County Clerk's office (Morristown, N.J.) There, we embarked on a quasi-professional Title Searching career with the much-welcomed cooperation of some experienced individuals. Having acquired the fundamental techniques of Deed Searching, we were ableto accelerate the pace of research. However, we were often thwarted by false leads, inferior or incomplete boundary descriptions or deeds which failed to record previous transactions. Fortunately, we discovered two invaluable Plat maps which depicted the individual tracts and their owners. They show the transformations which occurred from the time of George H. Danforth in 1887 (he owned most of the present FDU campus, at one time) to the extensive acreage (920) purchased by Hamilton Mc K. Twombly from 1890 to 1910."

Between 1868 and 1881, George W. Danforth purchased a number of land parcels that eventually were sold to Hamilton Twombly to become the heart of the Florham estate and now the Florham campus. Although Twombly made thirty-seven individual purchases of land parcels in 1890, the largest by far was bought from Danforth's widow, Emmeline. That sale comprised approximately 230 acres for a price of $130,000.

Other sizeable purchases include 19.32 acres from Jonathan and Julia L. Dwight for $45,000 in 1890, and 40 acres from Benjamin W. Burnet for $5,500, In 1893, Twombly exchanged five acres for four with the Sisters of Charity to correct a crooked boundary.

All of this assembled land gave Olmsted and his successors a sizeable holding when it came time to create one of America's most significant estates.

Convincing Hamilton Twombly

Olmsted's convincing of Hamilton Twombly was not a simple yes or no. The process took several steps and went through periods of uncertainty that lasted several years. Twombly had been consulting Sanford White of the prominent architectural firm of McKim, Mead & White about plans for additions to the Danforth property. (White's firm eventually designed and built the Mansion and other structures of Florham.) Olmsted and his stepson, John Charles, visited the property in mid-1890 and prepared plans for the grounds, but they were skeptical, urging Twombly to build "a large house on the hill on the other side of the railroad."

Olmsted explained Twombly's indecision in a March 3, 1981 letter to McKim, Mead & White, stating that "Twombly has decided so many time before to build his new house, and then returned to the scheme of altering the old one" that he would have to continuing making plans for the Danforth property.

A month later Olmsted wrote to Twombly that it would "be extremely difficult to make the old Danforth place a satisfactory country residency for you," noting that White agreed, and adding "there is a fundamental mistake in your plan of trying to make one good place out of two or three that apart are unsatisfactory." He emphasized that Twombly would be disappointed and that, to realize the home he wanted, he would have to take advantage of the extensive grounds of his land holdings.

Even though Twombly didn't make a final decision to proceed with Florham until June 29, 1893, at the end of 1891 he requested that Mead, McKim & White consult with Olmsted to determine a placing of the "new house" that was eventually built. Tentative plans were made for the location of the Mansion, the carriage house, the approaches, and other elements of the estate.

During this period of uncertainty about the creation of the estate, construction of the farm buildings—barns, stable, blacksmith shop, wagon shop, houses—was taking place on the rear section of Twombly's tract.

Mr. F. L. Olmsted,

Brookline, Mass.

Dear Mr. Olmsted:-

Your frank expression of opinion regarding my
property at Madison is appreciated in the spirit in which you have
made it, and it leads me to answer you as frankly regarding the
same subject. As you know, my first intention was to alter the
Danforth place, so as to make the house large enough to give us the
room we required, and to use the park property as an adjunct, where
I could have such a development as would make the whole place interesting, though not grand. Your positive opinion that the only
place to build a house was on the park property made a great im-
pression upon me, and I yielded to your better judgment so far as
to lay out the park, in view of possibly building a house there.
After adopting the plan suggested by you, it seemed to me that you
lost interest in the subject, and gave the matter very little personal attention, which led me to think that the plan was to your
mind simply the best way to get over something which was not capable of any very creditable result. For instance, the garden
having been placed near the track, your son stated that it was made
a certain size simply to get as large a garden as it was possible
to get. The roads were ballasted fourteen feet wide, and now it
is suggested that they should be made sixteen feet wide. The plan
of treating the valley was undecided, and the work on the valley
was allowed to go on.

As a result of all these annoyances, I was- and naturally--
discouraged, especially as there did not seem to be any definite
plan adopted for carrying out your ideas. With the experience you
have had, you must realize that, while it is a pleasure to see work
progressing in a systematic way, and results being obtained, even
if the expenditure is large, it is very unsatisfactory to see
everything disorganized, and money wasted which might easily be
saved; and, in the end, I might find that I had spent a large
amount of money on the land, and have an unsatisfactory place.

I have great confidence and respect for your advice and
taste, and would gladly follow the same, but I do not feel that I
have had the benefit of your personal judgment, and I am certain
if you realize the position, you would not be surprised at my con-
clusion; for I feel that if the organization of carrying out the
work, and the results of the progress made, were satisfactory to
you personally, they would also be so to me. I realize how many
large properties you have charge of, and I have thought that you
could not, perhaps, give me the time which the place required. If
I am wrong, I am only too glad to know it, as I feel that your
judgment is a prize to be wished for, if obtainable.

I trust you will take this letter in the same spirit you
have written me, and write me frankly upon the subject.

Mr. Burnett has just been here, and has reported to me his
favorable opinion of Mr. Riley. I should be very pleased to have
Mr. Riley take charge of the work, provided that he can be responsible to you for his plans, and can look to you for suggestions,
from time to time, as the work progresses.

Yours truly,

H. McK. Twombly

This letter of April 7, 1891 from Hamilton Twombly to Frederick Law Olmsted reveals some tension in the relationship between the two men over the question of where and how to begin. In the letter Twombly questions Olmsted's motives and stresses his discouragement at what he considered the disorganization and waste of money. He acknowledges that Olmsted is busy with the design of many large properties, but asks for more personal attention. Fortunately, these early "annoyances" were overcome and Florham was designed and created.

25

Creating the Florham Landscape

Beyond Hamilton Twombly's uncertainty about where to build his estate and his somewhat rocky relationship with Frederick Law Olmsted, realizing a beautiful landscape of contoured lawns, abundant trees, and colorful foliage required much more than an agreement to proceed. Many members of the Olmsted firm devoted hours to land surveys and the potential placement of buildings, trees, and gardens. In the early years of the 1890s, they developed Olmsted's concepts. After 1893, when he was no longer as active participant at Florham, his successors moved ahead with his ideas and their own. Fortunately, Olmsted, in addition to his eye for design, had an eye for talent, assembling a group who became the leaders of American landscape architecture in the twentieth century.

The Olmsted firm in the initial years had the complication of planning for two estates—the Danforth property and the acreage that would be Florham. Those plans must have played a part in helping Twombly decide between the two alternatives, along with Olmsted's urging.

As a first step topographical surveys of the two places were prepared to provide a detailed perspective of the features the landscape planners had to work with and any obstacles to be overcome. Once the firm understood what existed, Olmsted and his staff drew up plans to shape and enhance its features, along with the great need to clear wild growth and drain swampland. The process took most the last decade of the nineteeth century.

Even after the estate opened in 1897, it still was not finished. Gardens were created, more trees and foliage planted, a Madison Avenue entrace and railroad tunnel built, and additional buildings constructed.

Florham existed as the Vanderbilt-Twombly estate until Ruth Twombly's death in 1954 and the sale of the property in two phases—the farm property to ESSO (later EXXON) in 1955 and the 180 acres of the residential area to Fairleigh Dickinson University in 1957. The conversion to a campus meant the addition of new classrooms, library, recreatiional, and dormitory buildings and the replacement of several structures from the estate. Still, visitors to the campus will continue to experience the stamp of genius provided by Frederick Law Olmsted, his expert staff, and his significant successors.

Note that originals for the surveys and plans in this section, along with the photograph, may be found in the Olmsted archives in Brookline, Massachusetts.

Topographical Surveys before Construction

Because Hamilton Twombly took three years to decide which property to develop—Danforth or what became Florham—Olmsted's firm prepared topographical surveys of both in 1890 under the supervision of John Rowlett Brinley. The drawing below depicts the Danforth property and the drawing on the following page the land for Florham.

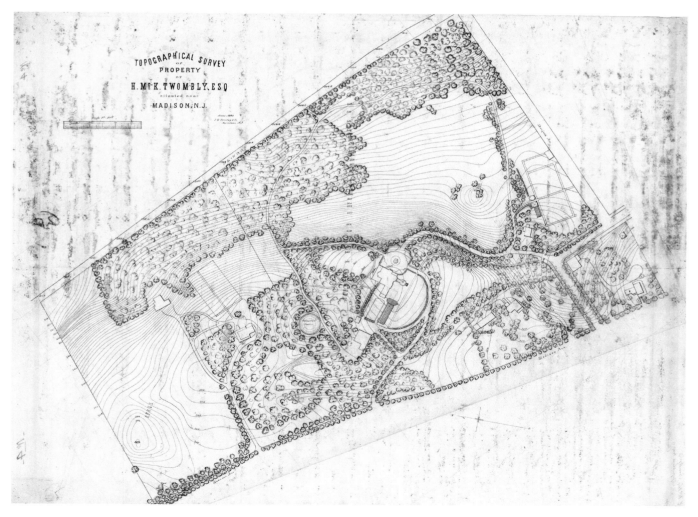

Madison Avenue in Madison, New Jersey, marks the lower boundry of both properties. The present Danforth Road is indicated on the right of the Danforth drawing, with railroad tracks diagonal at the top. The existing Danforth mansion is noted. Land owned by the Sisters of Charity is designated as "Convent" to the left of the Florham drawing. Both drawings show trees, contours, roads, and water.

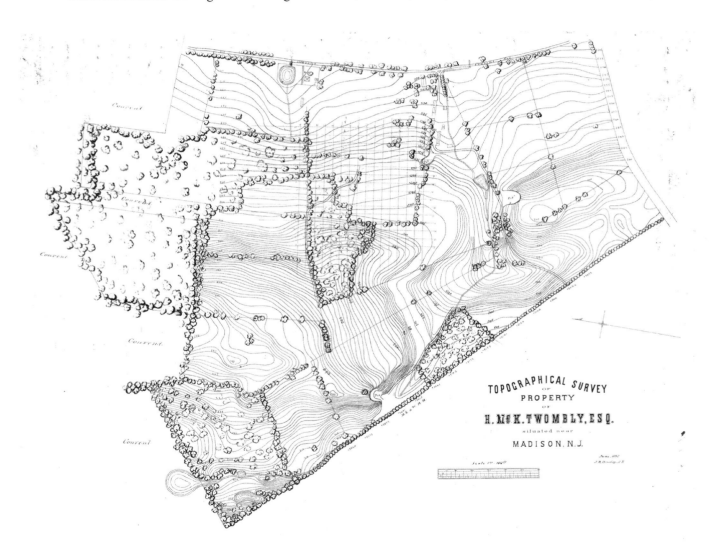

TOPOGRAPHICAL SURVEY
OF
PROPERTY
OF
H. McK. TWOMBLY, ESQ.
situated near
MADISON, N.J.

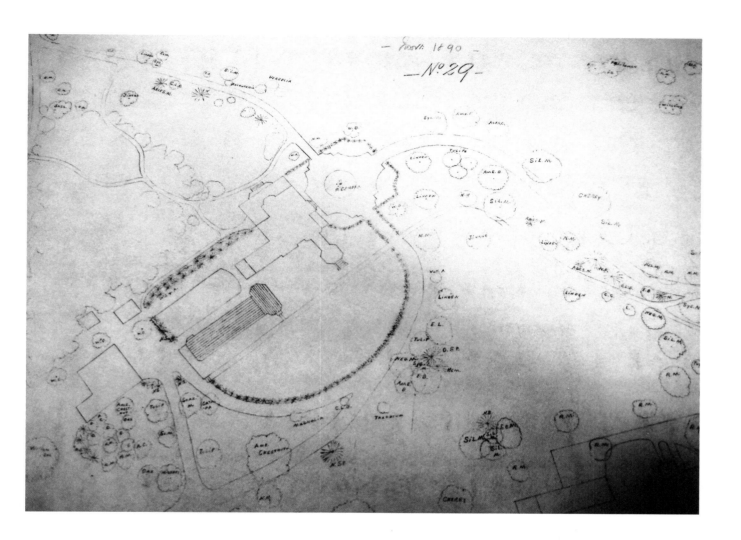

This 1890 drawing of the Danforth property shows the placement of the Mansion, roads, and trees. It provides a more detailed depiction of the area indicated in the center of the topographical survey of that year.

To the right of the large tree grouping, the close red lines on this topographical drawing of the Florham property from 1892 indicate the hill behind the future site of the Mansion and the rear gardens leading down to Park Avenue.

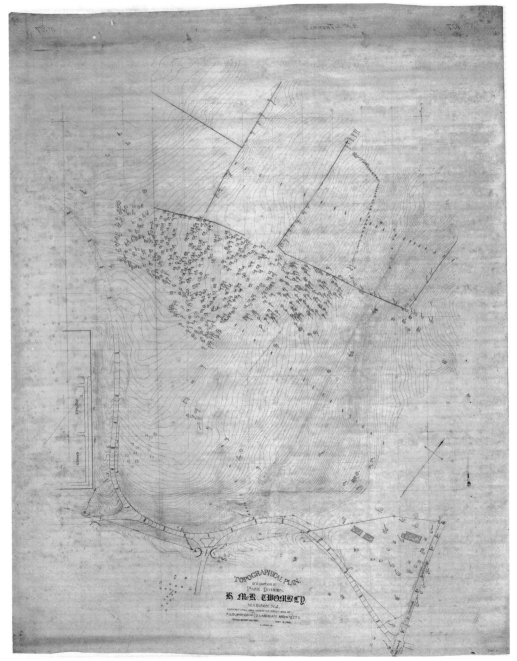

Planning and Clearing

From October 1890 until early 1891, the Olmsted firm provided layouts of the landscape on the Florham site, including designs for the South Hill, for the Park Division (the area west of the Mansion), for the Autumn Garden, and finally for the siting of the Mansion and other structures. While these plans were modified, the process typifies Olmsted's method for embodying his vision.

By the time Florham opened officially in 1897, its rolling topgraphy featured several hills, one 380 feet above sea level. More than 150 acres were wooded with walnut, chestnut, and oak trees, along for many unique and imported species. A fence of cypress pickets encircled the park around the Mansion.

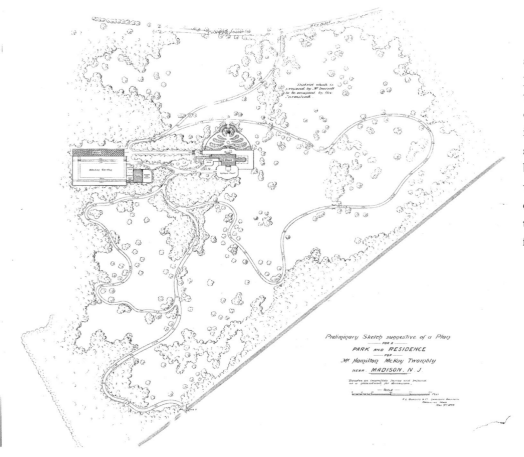

Preliminary Sketch suggestive of a Plan
FOR A
PARK AND RESIDENCE
FOR
Mr Hamilton McKay Twombly
NEAR MADISON. N J.

This preliminary sketch from 1890 does provide a location for the Mansion but includes a kitchen garden in the area where the stables were eventually built and projects a network of roadways very different from those that became part of the final estate.

The Mansion site selected by Olmsted overlooked a large overgrown and marshy acreage that had become infested with snakes and turtles.

After a survey by landscape architect J.R. Brinley, the two-year process of clearing brush and draining the swamp began at a cost of $100,000. Hundreds of Italian laborers were brought across the Atlantic to carry out the physical work. A number were retained in future years as groundkeepers for the estate.

This 1892 photograph looking from the railroad tracks to Madison Avenue shows the condition of the terrain before clearing.

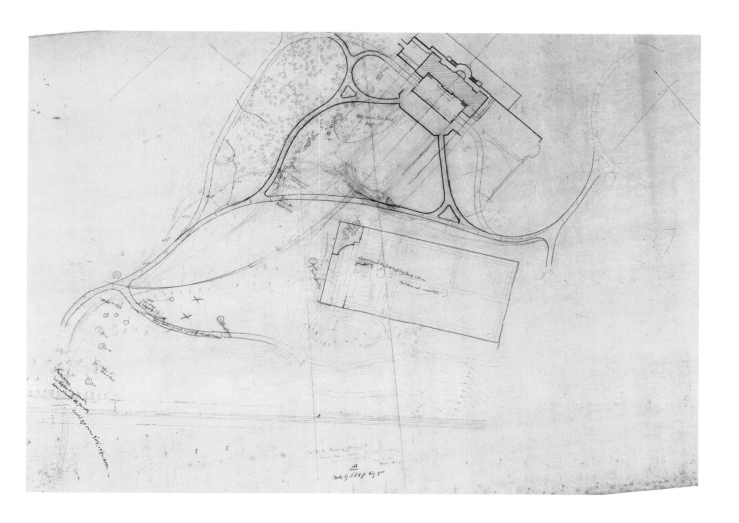

This preliminary plan for a new forecourt for the mansion was prepared to address Hamilton Twombly's concerns regarding delivery traffic to the front of the building. Some of the red lines indicate ideas for the placement of access roads. The penciled area suggests a new large forecourt. The red-lined rectangle in the center of the drawing indicates the site for greenhouses and gardens. Compare this plan with the 1896 lawn grade drawing (see following page) to see how it was modified.

This 1896 lawn grade drawing prepared a year before the estate opened shows all that had been built and installed up to this point. The vegetable garden and greenhouses are on the upper left, the stables to the center right, and the Mansion in the middle, with the lines indicating the hill down to Park Avenue indicated by gray lines. Note that the final road approaches to the Mansion still have not been determined.

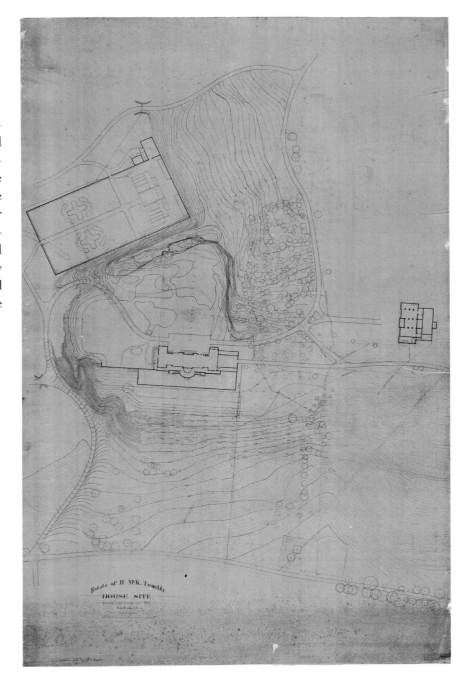

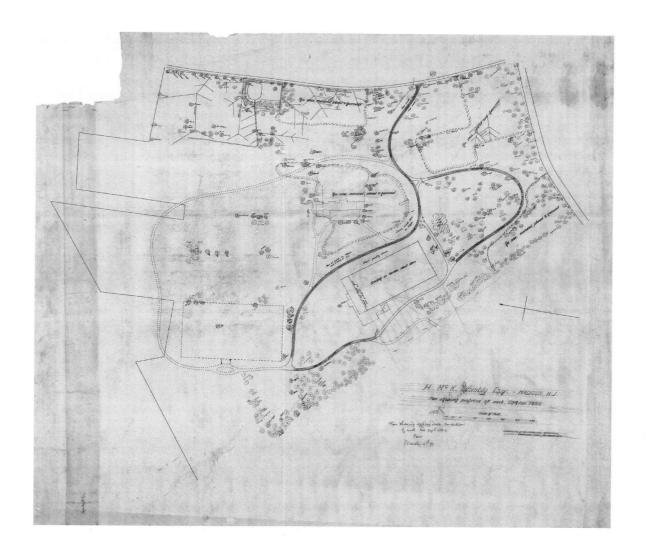

This progress plan was prepared in response to Hamilton Twombly's letter to Olmsted complaining about an apparent lack of progress. It depicts the area being worked on, including what would become the garden and greenhouses beneath the brown line for the road that leads to Park Avenue, which is near the top of the drawing according to this view.

This 1892 planting plan depicts the area around the greenhouses and the vegetable garden below them. Note the square in the middle of the greenhouse shapes. That is the proposed location of the palm house, which finally was built in an area to the left of the greenhouses. The line to the left of the drawing indicates the railroad tracks. The list of plants in the upper right covers the eventual site of the stables.

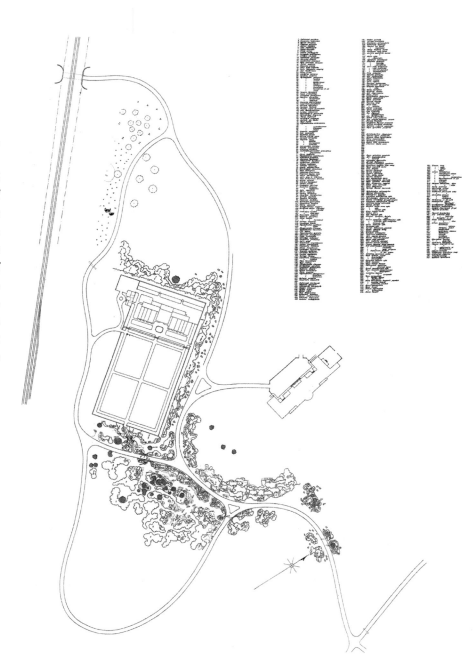

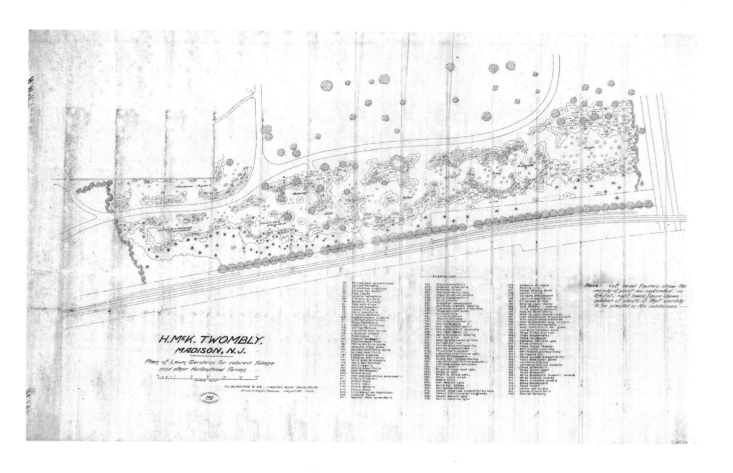

This lawn garden and colored foliage plan from 1892 was developed for the area east of the railroad tracks, with Danforth Road to the right. The shape to the upper left depicts a wall corner that still stands. This area is the site of the existing maple grove, now indicated by a Friends of Florham marker noting Olmsted's role in the planting. The details of the elaborate design show numbers keyed to the list of plants and flowers that would fulfill Olmsted's vision of color for that part of the estate.

**Olmsted topographical tree plan of 1892
superimposed over photograph of present
Florham**

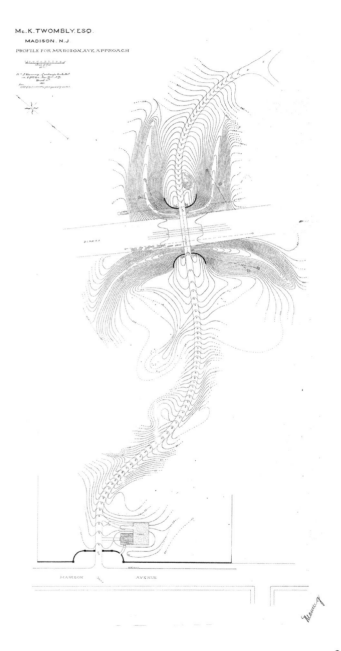

William S. Manning, in 1898, after the estate was open and occupied by the Vanderbilt-Twomblys, prepared this plan for the present Madison Avenue entrance. He was probably assisted by John Rowlett Brinley, with whom he shared a New York office address. Brinley contributed to the design of the tunnel under the railroad tracks.

The Changing Landscape of Florham

**Railroad to
Madison Avenue
1892**

Railroad tunnel to Madison Avenue 1935

Railroad tunnel to Madison Avenue 2018

OLMSTED'S SUCCESSORS AT FLORHAM

After encouraging the creation of Florham as a grand estate and participating in the initial land-scaping design, Frederick Law Olmsted ceased daily involvement in 1893 to concentrate his efforts on Biltmore and The Columbia Exposition. Because of failing health and the early stages of dementia, he retired completely in 1895. Further development of the landscaping plan and the fulfillment of his vision was left to the Olmsted Company, now in the hands of his stepson, John Charles, his son Frederick, Jr., and Henry Sargent Codman. With the untimely death of Codman, Charles Eliot became a partner in 1897.

From 1890 to 1896, assisting directly for the Olmsted group were John Rowlett Brinley (an independant CE), George Cooke, Warren H. Manning, William S. Manning, Horatio Buckenham, Henry Sargent Codman, and Percival Gallagher. The Olmsted firm returned sporadically in future years, with Percivval Gallagher designing the azalea garden in 1928. Additionally, the Manning brothers, Brinley, and others had independent roles in the establishment of the Florham landscape.

The American Society of Landscape Architects

In 1899, Warren Manning wrote to Charles Eliot seeking assistance in creating a professional organization for landscape architects. Eliot was more interested in a public association, which culminated in the forma-tion of the American Civic Association. After this organization's founding, Manning, turning to the Olmsted brothers for help, formed the American Society of Landscape Architects. The eleven charter members met for the first time in 1899 in New York City.

Although Frederick Law Olmsted was no longer active and played no direct role in the ASLA's cre-ation, the Society represents an embodiment of his vision to establish landscape architecture as a distin-guished profession.

Today, ASLA is the national professional association representing landscape architects, with more than 16,000 members in all 50 states, U.S. territories, and 42 countries around the world, plus more than 70 student chapters. From its beginning, the group had a mission to "establish landscape architecture as a rec-ognized profession in North America," "develop educational studies in landscape architecture," and "provide a voice of authority in the 'New Profession.'"

The Olmsted Brothers

Frederick Law Olmsted fully recognized his genius and the revolution he had brought about in landscape design. Near the end of his life, he wrote to a friend: "I have raised my calling from the rank of a trade, even a handicraft, to that of a liberal profession—an Art, an Art of Design. I have been resolute in insisting that I am not to be dealt with as an agent of my clients, but as a councillor (sic)—a trustee in honor."

John Charles Olmsted

Olmsted had created an extraordinarily successful firm, with commissions all over the United States, and as he grew older was intent on grooming his two sons to take over his firm and continue his work. In the Spring of 1895, on a trip to Asheville, North Carolina to inspect the landscape work proceeding at George Vanderbilt's new estate, Biltmore, Olmsted, at the age of 63, began to experience, and acknowledge, the first signs of Alzheimer's, or some variation of senile dementia, a progressive disease which necessitated him being sent to an institution for care in 1898. It was that year that his stepson, John, at the age of 46, and his son Frederick Jr, age 28—who shared some of his father's unique ability to conceptualize landscapes—created the successor firm, Olmsted Brothers.

Olmsted Brothers, and its team of specialists, continued work on ongoing commissions, including Biltmore and Florham, and over the next decades would continue the high standards set by Frederick Law Olmsted, with a host of projects throughout the country, including park systems, universities, exposition grounds, libraries, hospitals, residential neighborhoods and state capitols. Some of the notable work of Olmsted Brothers included roads in the Great Smoky mountains, Arcadia National Parks, Yosemite Valley and Atlanta's Piedmont Park; park systems in Portland, Seattle, Atlanta and Boston; and residential neighborhoods in Oak Bay, British Columbia. At Duke University, the firm designed the grounds of part of the University, mapping large trees around proposed buildings

Frederick Olmsted, Jr.

and planting 52 species of trees on the campus. Olmsted Brothers was by far the largest landscape architecture practice in the United States in the early twentieth century. As with Frederick Law Olmsted, Olmsted Brothers focus was on picturesque landscape design to create a sense of peace and awareness of nature, using different species of trees, of different heights, using open spaces, and featuring light and shadow to bring out the inherent beauty of the landscape.

Frederick Law Olmsted died in 1903 at the age of 81, but Olmsted Brothers would continue on maintaining his high standards, even after John's death in 1920 and Frederick Jr's retirement in 1949 and death in 1957. The firm under the Olmsted name in fact continued in business until 2000.

Warren H. Manning

Frederick Law Olmsted's reputation as a landscape architect was so towering that he attracted the very best talent eager to work with him. One of his most important associates was William H. Manning. Manning was born in Massachusetts in 1860; his father owned and operated a nursery and took him on many botanical expeditions, as well as visits to other nurseries. His mother was an artist, a water colorist, who heightened her son's awareness of the beauty of the natural world. It was therefore not surprising that Manning decided to pursue garden design as his profession.

Hoping to associate himself with "the most eminent man in the landscape profession," Manning in 1885 joined the office of Frederick Law Olmsted. He worked as part of Olmsted's team that landscaped the thousands of acres of the Biltmore Estate being developed by Florence Vanderbilt Twombly's youngest brother, George, in Asheville, North Carolina, and during the next eight years worked with Olmsted on 125 projects in twenty-two states, including Olmsted's ongoing work at Florham.

Manning's special interest was in naturalistic landscaping, seeing what the landscape as he found it had to offer, and then enhancing the beauty that he saw, rather than trying to impose a formalistic design on the landscape. Manning used native plants that required little maintenance and strove to preserve and enhance the naturalistic settings he could see.

In 1893, due to problems between Olmsted and Hamilton Twombly, Manning did private work for the Twombly's. In 1896, Manning, having been passed over as a partner in favor of Charles Elliot, left the Olmsted firm after eight years of service.

William S. Manning

William S. Manning worked for the Olmsted firm with his brother Warren H. Their father, Jacob Warren Manning, was a prize-winning horticulturalist, who developed new species of fruits and ornamental plants. Plants from his nursery went to nearly every state in the Union and many foreign countries. His son William S. served as landscape manager of Florham for a period in the 1890s because of his understanding of Olmsted's working methodology and aesthetic goals. He left Florham in 1899 to become superintendent of the Essex County, New Jersey, park system, which had been developed by the Olmsted Brothers. In 1906, he took charge of Baltimore, Maryland, parks, another Olmsted Brothers project. He maintained that role until 1917 when the general superintendent position was eliminated. William S. Manning died in Massachusetts on April 8, 1926.

Horatio Buckenham

Another of the stars of the Olmsted Firm was Horatio Buckenham, who has been called "a genius of landscape architecture." In 1875, Buckenham started out as a draftsman for Olmsted Sr. Olmsted firmly believed in, and fostered, apprenticeship and mentoring within his organization. Buckenham was an excellent example of his tutelage. Buckenham left the Olmsted firm in 1897 and formed Buckenham and Miller. In addition to work at "Florham," Buckenham in 1900 took over the design work for the grounds of Duke Farms, the 2,700 acre estate in Hillsborough, New Jersey acquired by James Buchanan Duke, the founder of American Tobacco Company—at the time the largest manufacturer of cigarettes in the world—and Duke Power Company. For seven years, Buckenham worked on this project, leading a team of 1,200 men to lay out rolling hills, nine lakes, 18 miles of roads and meandering nature paths, reservoirs, bridges, gardens with statuary and fountains, importing from Europe one shipment of 60,000 trees, and another of 20,000 blue spruce, spending over $400,000 a year to create a naturalistic romantic landscape that captured his client's vision as well as his own.

Percival Gallagher

Percival Gallagher met Frederick Law Olmsted, Jr. while he was studying at Harvard's fine arts program. In 1894, upon graduation at the age of 20, Gallagher joined Frederick Law Olmsted's firm, where his knowledge of horticulture meshed with his sense of beauty was put to good use on such commissions as the continuing work at Florham, and with the restoration of the plants around the U.S. Capitol in Washington, D.C.

Ten years later, he broke off to start his own landscape architecture firm, but two years later re-joined Olmsted Brothers and as made a partner in 1927. Some of his well-known projects included the landscape at a number of colleges including Bryn Mawr, Haverford, Swarthmore, Vassar and Duke University, as well as the development of the park system in Essex County and Union County, New Jersey.

George Cooke

Born in Surrey, England in 1849, George Cooke had no formal training in horticulture or landscape architecture, but rather received his education on the job, working as a gardener at some of Great Britain's great estate's and at the famous Royal Botanical Gardens, Kew, where he developed some hybrid species. Cooke immigrated to the United States in 1895 and first worked in New Jersey at the Twomblys' "Florham" estate. The work on the landscape was winding down in 1896 with the Twomblys first occupying Florham in the spring of 1897. Cooke moved on to work at the New York City Department of Public Parks, where he met the landscape architect and New York City parks official, Samuel Parsons, Jr., forming a partnership with him. The partnership is best known for developing the San Diego city parks, after which Cooke and Parsons received many commissions in the San Diego area.

John Rowlett Brinley

John Rowlett Brinley, (born in Perth Amboy, New Jersey in 1861), a graduate of from Columbia University School of Mines, in civil engineering. He started receiving small commissions as a landscape architect in 1885. In 1890, Frederick Law Olmsted Sr. engaged Brinley to do the survey for Florham, and supervise the clearing of brush and draining of the swamps. An unfortunate set back was a fire that destroyed his office and records, resulting in him losing this commission. Hwe began working directly for the Twomblys to design and oversee the construction of the Madison Ave. entrance and tunnel. In 1901, with a fellow graduate, John Swift Holbrook, he organized the firm of Brimley and Holbrook, landscape engineers and architects. They maintained offices in Morristown, New Jersey, and New York City. The focus of Brinley's work was creating landscape plans for estates of the wealthy in New Jersey, New York and Connecticut, working also on parks, schools and hospitals throughout the Northeast. Brinley often partnered with larger landscape firms. While these firms largely followed the picturesque or romantic school of landscape design, popularized by the Olmsted firm, Brinley preferred a more traditional and formal approach to his personal designs. Some of his well-known projects included the New York Botanical Gardens, the Morristown Green, and Florham.

FLORHAM'S ORNAMENTAL GARDENS

This photograph of the Mansion in the early 1900s reveals that initially the house followed the example of English country houses with an expanse of lawn and a lack of trees, shrubs, flowers, and other foliage. But within a decade after the estate opened, elaborate gardens were constructed to the side and rear of the building, and trees and shrubs were added to the front lawn.

A section of the 1910 Florham Park map of the Twombly property indicates that the name Italian Garden refers to both the present garden of that name and to the garden and fountain behind the Mansion. The greenhouses and sunken (vegetable) garden are on the left. The building drawn under the word "Green" is the palm house, which was torn down when the Orangerie was constructed.

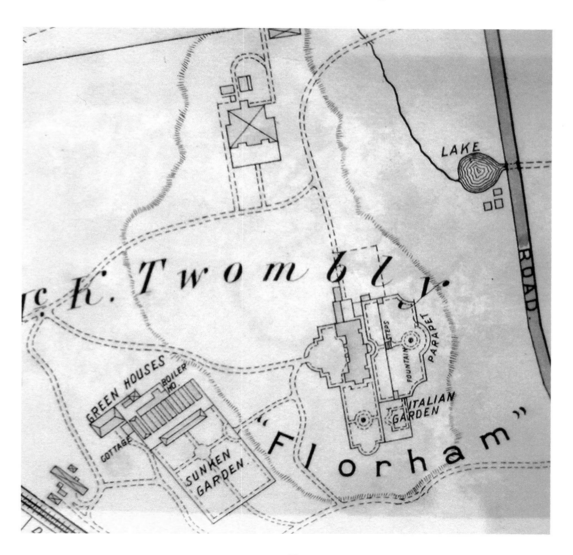

"Costly Ornamental Gardens"

These words began an article in *The Jerseyman* newspaper of July 31, 1908, on the construction of the gardens around the "Florham" Mansion. In late November of the previous year, it was announced that the English landscape architect Alfred Parsons had been engaged by Hamilton Twombly to plan the gardens adjoining his residence. "...[T]he completed garden will be one of the finest in the country," *The Jerseyman's* readers were informed.

This 1908 article describes in some detail the implementation of the garden plan: the massive walls, the ornamental pools and stairways, and handsome gazebos which still adorn this impressive garden landscape.

Here is the article as it appeared in *The Jerseyman*:

COSTLY ORNAMENTAL GARDENS
Improvements on the Twombly Estate will add to its beauty.

The largest piece of work now going on in the building line in this vicinity is the new garden for H. McK. Twombly, on which Sturgis Bros. have a considerable force of men employed, while laborers are busily moving the large amount of earth necessary for the completion of the plans.

Sturgis Bros. are putting up a terrace wall which will require about eighteen hundred yards of concrete. The wall at the highest point, including foundation, is twenty-six feet high, and at the bottom of the concrete is seven feet wide. It is built on a batter, the forms being constructed of worked lumber with the face oiled to give a better surface to the wall.

In addition, there are two handsome garden houses of brick and cut stone at either end of the upper terrace and two ornamental pools are also being constructed, ornamental stairways and gates adding to the effectiveness. The east garden has been remodelled and considerable new cut stone put in, and at present masons are engaged in laying a large amount of concrete walk. A.S. Pierson is superintending the work.

ARTHUR CLARKE HERRINGTON

It was Frederick Law Olmsted whose vision created the Florham landscape, but the work he began was refined by a succession of talented horticulturists.

Hamilton Twombly was able to entice to Florham the head gardener from Queen Victoria's Kew Gardens: Arthur Clarke Herrington. Herrington began his work at Florham in 1896, appointed Superintendent/Gardener, and was in charge of the large complex of greenhouses and conservatories. He lived in a house in Madison, several blocks east of Florham, on Fairview Avenue. It was not until the Spring of 1897 that the Twomblys first occupied Florham; the hiring of Herrington in 1896 is further evidence of how committed Hamilton Twombly was to the horticultural aspects of his country estate.

From all accounts, this distinguished-looking Englishman was a man of great vigor, intensity and good humor who endeared himself to the local garden club ladies with his charm, and had a field day using Florham as his laboratory to grow award-winning plants and to create hybrid varieties.

Several of the Florham greenhouses were devoted to orchids, Mrs. Twombly's favorite flower. An exquisite specimen would be set before her place setting at every breakfast, lunch and dinner throughout her long life. The orchids which filled the greenhouses were imported from their countries of origin in South America, Central America, and the Caribbean, and from Mexico and India; Herrington would propagate and cross breed them to create new varieties.

Another greenhouse was devoted to another of Mrs. Twombly's favorites: chrysanthemums. The chrysanthemums grown at Florham were known internationally. In 1904, the Mikado's gardener, the Garden Architect for Imperial Japan, came to tour the Florham greenhouses and see for himself the new species developed by Arthur Herrington. And *The American Florist* of November 10, 1906, reported that Herrington was preparing to ship a "five bush specimen with over 500 flowers on it" to the Chicago Flower Show.

Herrington won numerous medals for plants and flower arrangements at various exhibitions, as well as awards and prizes for his work, including: Prize Winner at Madison Square Garden & Boston

Shows of November 1897; Prize Winner for chrysanthemums at the New York Show of November 1900; Prize winner at Newport in September of 1903, and Boston Show Winner for chrysanthemums in November of 1904. In 1905, Herrington published the definitive work on chrysanthemums, titled *Chrysanthemum: Its Culture for Professionals and Amateurs*, a study which is still in print today.

In his work in the Florham greenhouses, Herrington created other hybrid species. One, which he brought out in 1901, was a new Gerbera, the "Barbarton Daisy," which was called "the most unique and beautiful plant that has been placed before the public during the past ten years." It received the first prize at the Grand Horticultural Exhibition at the New York Botanical Gardens that year as the best horticultural novelty in America. It is also believed that Herrington in 1903 created a chrysanthemum given the name "Mrs. H. McK. Twombly," described as a "white shaded pink; a fine early variety."

In 1899, Herrington created a new hybrid daylily, which he registered under the name "Florham"—"Hemerocallis Florham," This lily, three to four feet in height, had canary yellow blossoms that were six inches in diameter, with petals four inches long, one and a quarter inches broad, and brightened the Twomblys' herbaceous borders and parterres. It was said to be the first American daylily hybrid. It was frequently used thereafter in hybridizing work, and many present-day varieties are clearly genetic descendants of their Florham ancestor. The Florham daylily was related to a species known to be growing at that time in the Royal Botanic Gardens at Kew, England, undoubtedly a species with which Herrington was familiar when he began his work at Florham.

In 1997, the Friends of Florham began their search for the long lost Florham daylily, consulting with the top experts in the country. All were familiar with it, but none knew where a specimen could be found. One suggested contacting a nursery in Tennessee, only to learn that their stock had died out a few years before and no records existed of its whereabouts. The Garden Club of America reported the search on its website and growers across the country were contacted, until finally it was located at a daylily farm in Vermont and brought to Florham to grace the gardens around the Mansion.

After Hamilton Twombly died on January 10, 1910, Herrington resigned from Florham. He remained active both nationally and internationally as a frequent lecturer, and for twenty-five years was the manager of the prestigious International Flower Show in New York City.

The brilliant gardens so essential to the character of Florham—as the photographs at the beginning of this chapter reveal--did not exist until decades after the estate opened as the country home of the Vanderbilt-Twomblys. The first of these gardens, the Italian Garden, was created in 1907, and a year later, the garden was expanded to the grounds at the rear of the Mansion. Both were designed by Alfred Parsons, working with Arthur Clarke Herrington.

ALFRED PARSONS

It was reported in *The Jerseyman* of November 29, 1907, that "H. McK. Twombly is having a fine Italian garden constructed adjoining his residence at Florham from plans by an English architect, Mr. Parsons. The work will approximate $50,000 in cost, and it is expected that the completed garden will be one of the finest in the country."

Why 1907? Why did the Twomblys' decide to create this garden next to the Mansion in 1907? Their only son, Hamilton Twombly Jr., had died the summer before, on July 5, 1906, in a tragic drowning accident, a loss which devastated the family. Might this new garden—so close to the Mansion—have been planned as a memorial tribute to Hamilton Jr.?

The Mr. Parsons referred to in that news clip was sixty-year-old Alfred Parsons, an English botanical illustrator, landscape painter, and garden designer. Garden designing grew out of his work as an artist, and almost all of his commissions were in England and Scotland, where it was believed that an artist could design better gardens. Parson's work in the United States was limited, with Florham as one of his projects. It is possible that Twombly knew of Parsons through John Singer Sargent, who painted Florence Twombly in 1890 and, like Parsons, was a member of the Broadway Group of artists in England.

This garden, which included a parterre, a pergola, gravel walks and statues standing atop the encircling wall, could be admired from the Drawing Room of the Mansion, from the terrace, and from Mrs. Twombly's bedroom windows.

In 1997, the Friends of Florham restored these gardens which were dedicated at a Sunday in May at a ceremony which included a tribute to the hundreds of workmen—chiefly immigrant Italians—who supplied the labor that helped to make Parsons' garden design a spectacular reality. Frances Mantone, a granddaughter of one of those workmen, Anthony Pico, expressed the gratitude of the area's Italian-American community for the Friends' and the University's recognition of "those hard-working people, diligent and conscientious, who came to America for a better life . . . with very little except their deep commitment to their families and their love of the earth."

Several of the plantings in the re-created parterre—some peonies, columbine, and irises, for instance—are survivors from the original garden designed by Parsons in 1907 and supervised by Herrington thereafter.

Italian Garden
Designed in 1907 by
Alfred Parsons

**Italian Garden
May 30, 1939**

Italian Garden in bloom 2016

Rose garden
that at one time
existed to the rear
of the Mansion

Fountain
to the rear
of the Mansion
in the 1950s

Aerial view of the rear garden today

Mansion
back garden
from pergola
in the 1950s

FLORHAM'S FLOWERS AND FRUITS

Florence and Hamilton Twombly's greenhouses, mainly devoted to the cultivation of chrysanthemums and orchids, were well known in horticultural circles in the early 20th century. The Twomblys' amazing horticultural center, said at the time to consist of "24,000 running feet of greenhouse," was overseen by Arthur Herrington, an Englishman lured from the Royal Botanical society in 1896. Herrington, who died in 1950, managed the gardens and flower culture until Hamilton Twombly's death in 1910. In the following years, he went on to become one of America's leading horticulturists.

Some years ago, the Friends of Florham received an inquiry from the Reynolda Gardens of Wake Forest University in Winston-Salem regarding the existence of a day lily called "Florham," noted in Reynolda's original planting lists. Research on the flower now shows that Arthur Herrington developed this cultivar in 1899. Experts in the day lily community have stated that the "Florham," described as having "petals four inches long, one and one-quarter inches broad and of a clear canary-yellow color," played an important role in the development of other cultivars.

Other cultivars were apparently introduced by the Twombly greenhouses. One of them brought out in 1901 by Herrington was a new Gerbera, the "Barbarton Daisy," once said "to be the most unique and beautiful plant that has been placed before the public during the past ten years." It received the first prize at the Grand Horticultural Exhibition at the New York Botanical Gardens that year as the best horticultural novelty in America. Another flower that was quite likely developed at Florham was a chrysanthemum listed in a 1903 catalogue of Peter Henderson & Co. of New York. Given the name "Mrs. H. McK. Twombly," it is described as a "white shaded pink; a fine early variety." Though the fact is not positively established, the "Mrs. Twombly" plant is in all probability an Arthur Herrington creation in light of his authority as a propagator and grower of mums.

The Florham lily was the most famous of the new flowers bred by the estate's gardeners. It was registered under the name "Florham" in 1899 by Arthur Herrington, an internationally recognized gardening expert. Herrington introduced it as a then-brand-new cross between "hemerocallis aurantiaca major," and "hemerocallis Thunbergii." It soon became the ancestor of numbers of the nation's lily varieties.

A Tyson floral arrangement

The "Mrs. H. McK. Twombly" chrysanthemum won prizes at a number of flower shows, in many cases receiving first place awards. Her gardener credited at these exhibits was R. Tyson. A 1917 issue of *Floriculture* reports that "In the center of: the hall, Robert Tyson, Superintendent for Mrs. H. McK. Twombly, exhibited a large group of chrysanthemum plants in flower, with foliage plants for effect. The group covered over 50 square feet of floor space and was carried up in pyramidal form. On each side of the quadrangle, small groups were placed."

Plants in the Orangerie

The Orangerie was constructed in the 1920s with skylights and large windows to provide an ideal environment for cultivation of both flowers and plants to supplement the greenhouses, which were the largest complex in New Jersey at the time .

Chef Donon took great pride in the fruits, vegetables, and flowers grown in the Orangerie and greenhouses: "From our greenhouses we could get melons the size of a small beach ball, and grapes the size of my thumb—one bunch would be a foot long! In the Orangerie we had every fruit—oranges, lemons, figs— everything. Mrs. Twombly told me that she only enjoyed vegetables at home. Even those at the Ritz Hotel in Paris were not as good as what we had at Florham. We got them fresh in the morning— right to the kitchen door. If I wanted something special or something changed, I would work through our office in New York and they would tell the gardener what to grow. Mrs. Twombly had a big greenhouse just for flowers; she really loved orchids—that was her flower. She had them on the table every day."

Flowers in the Orangerie

Florham greenhouses

One of the original green-houses, called the Palm House, towered sixty-four feet high and was topped by a huge dome. When the Orangerie was built, it was removed

Link to Bygone Splendor

FD Seeks Use for Old Twombly Tunnel

By JIM STAPLES
Staff Correspondent.

MADISON — To most persons it's just a hole in the ground, but to longtime employes at the Fairleigh Dickinson University campus here, a 900-foot tunnel is a link with bygone splendor.

Practical university overseers are still trying to find some use for the unusual tunnel.

"We've thought about using it as a bomb or fallout shelter, but it's quite near the surface, and it would need elaborate ventilation," a staff member said.

Most students are unaware of the tunnel's existence and university officials discourage student access, lest they dream up new uses for it.

"The tunnel was built in 1924 to carry steam pipes from the boiler room to the mansion," said John McVey, shining a light dov the six-foot square concrete passage.

Now overseer of heating facilities on the campus, McVey went to work there when it was the Twombly Estate. Those were the days when servants would carry bouquets of flowers through the tunnel, from a lavish greenhouse to the former Hamilton Twombly Mansion. The university bought the estate in 1958.

A locked door blocks entry to the tunnel at the power house. The mansion end exits into a cramped area beneath a sidewalk grill. Entry to the building is through a small sunken window.

"A few students have gotten into the tunnel from the mansion window, but after going 900 feet through the dark, they have come up against a locked steel door.

That's discouraged exploration," McVey said.

Was Show Place

In its heyday the estate, Florham Farms, was a national show place. Its 100-room mansion was built in the 1890s for a reported $2 million. Near the still-operating boiler building (former power house) were greenhouses where tropical trees were grown, and a tree shed, in which other delicate trees were put for the winter.

The Twombleys, who made their fortune in railroading spared no effort in maintaining the individuality of the estate.

Even the boilers were monogrammed. "Twombly" is handsomely cast into the ends of the two large heating units.

This news story from the *Newark Evening News* edition of May 2, 1962 explains how during the years of the Florham estate a tunnel served as the access to bring flowers from the Orangerie and the greenhouses to the Mansion. No doubt, that route was also used to bring produce to Chef Donon's kitchen.

FLORHAM'S VEGETABLE GARDENS

Chef Donon in his memoirs had written that the "vegetable gardens were on the Florham side, on the hill near Convent Station." From aerial shots of the estate during its Florham days, it is clear that there were gardens around the Orangerie, a logical place for a vegetable garden, but this was certainly not next to the Sisters of Charity land "on the hill near Convent Station."

From aerial photographs from each decade, it is evident that the area now occupied by the Wyndham Hamilton Park Hotel and its parking lot was under cultivation during Mrs. Twombly's reign, but after the University took over reverted to grass and scrub growth. In the aerial photographs before 1955, you can see the truck paths through this area where the trucks would have harvested the produce to bring to Chef Donon's kitchen door. Here were the vegetable gardens to which Donon referred.

1892 topographical survey of vegetable garden site overlaid on current photograph of the Wyndham hotel

The Mystery of Chef Donon's Mushroom Cave

In his memoirs, Chef Donon, describing how all of his ingredients came from the Florham Farm, the Orangerie, the greenhouses, and the vegetable gardens, wrote: "I asked them to build me a cave where we could grow mushrooms and other special things. I had them grow celery there —it was about half the size you see in the market now, but it was white as snow and very crisp. All of Mrs. Twombly's guests loved it and asked where she bought it. They couldn't believe that we grew it right there on the property."

This fleeting reference to a mushroom cave is the only written evidence of its existence. But it was recently rediscovered.

Near the campus Public Safety Building past the Black Box Theater, past the greenhouse, there, set in the north facing hillside, is a structure that looks like the front of a small chapel, made of a brownstone type of stone, and over the door, inscribed in the stone, the date: 1927.

Far from being a muddy hole, the mushroom cave is an elaborate structure, fitting of the way Mrs. Twombly did everything. It is approximately 60 feet in length, an enormous room, about twelve feet wide, the walls of stone perhaps three feet thick. The structure is now used for storage of housekeeping supplies and nothing seems to remain of the days of growing mushrooms and celery when perhaps there were planting tables. A good twelve feet above the concrete floor, there is an air vent with a very old fan inside which would draw air in through an air shaft on top of the hillside.

The Mushroom Cave was constructed in 1927, as indicated by the inscribed date. The door is not the original

THE PLANTINGS OF FLORHAM

Many of the shrubs and trees placed at Florham originally came from around the world, first imported to the United States in the late 1600's and early 1700s and later. Nurserymen then planted, propagated, and sold them. Plants used at Florham came from multiple sources, including the original Danforth Estate. Many nurseries from New Jersey, New York, Pennsylvania, Massachusetts, and even Illinois provided specimens, including some plants from nurseries that still exist today (i.e., Hicks, Moon).

These were the suppliers: Parsons and Sons Co. (Kissena Nurseries, Flushing, NY), S. C. Moon (Morrisville PA), W. H. Moon (Morrisville, PA), Thomas Meehan and Sons (Philadelphia, PA), H. H. Berger & Co. (NY, NY), Hoopes, Bro and Thomas Co. (The West Chester Nursery, West Chester, PA), F. G. Pratt (Concord Nursery, Concord, MA), Temple and Beard (Shady Hill Nursery, Cambridge, MA), C. Ribsam and Sons (Trenton, NJ), R. Douglas and Sons (Waukegan Nurseries, Waukegan IL), J. Dawson (Eastern Nurseries), Wm. C. Strong (Newton Highlands, MA), G. A. Parker (Parker and Wood (Boston, MA), L. M. Noe (Madison, NJ), Chas. A. Harkness.

What remains of the original trees and other plantings is uncertain. Many trees, however, that are original to Florham, can be attributed strictly on their size. As with all Gilded Age estates, the landscape of Florham was constantly in flux.

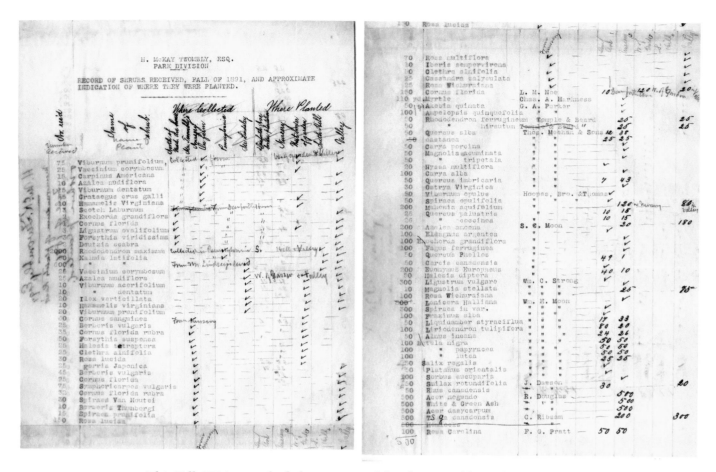

This Fall 1891 record of plants received for the Twombly Park Division with an indication of where they were planted included the number of each ordered and their souces. Some came from the Danforth property, some from an on-site nursery, and some from the farm. Others were ordered from a number of the nursery suppliers. Note that before the decision to build and landscape the Florham estate, the acreage was designated as the Park Division.

THE TREES OF FLORHAM

Sweet Gum
Smoke Tree
Japanese Holly
American Holly
Hybrid Holly
Red Beauty ®
Seven-son Flower
Burning Bush
Kousa Dogwood
Flowering Dogwood
Steller Pink Dogwood
Aurora Dogwood
Cornelian Cherry
Leyland Cyrpress
Japanese Cedar
Chinese Juniper
Eastern Red Cedar
Eastern Arborvitae
Black Walnut
Crape Myrtle
Southern Magnolia
Star Magnolia
Saucer Magnolia
American Linden
Tomentos Linden
Black Gum
White Fringe Tree
Japanese Tree Lilac
Concolr Fir
Nordmann Fir
Norway Spruce
Dwarf Alberta Spruce
Serbian Spruce

White Fringe Tree
Japanese Tree Lilac
Concolr Fir
Nordmann Fir
Norway Spruce
Dwarf Alberta Spruce
Serbian Spruce
Oriental Spruce
Skylands Oriental Spruce
Colorado Blue Spruce
Hoopsi Colorado Blue Spruce
Blue Atlas Cedar
Cedar of Lebanon
Vanderwolf Limber Pine
Swiss Mountain Pine
Eastern White Pine
Canadian Hemlock
Weeping Canadian Hemlock
Southern Japanese Hemlock
Eastern Arborvitae
Western Arborvitae
Oriental Arborvitae
Dawn Redwood
Russian Olive
Rainbow Coast Leucothoe
Japanese Scholor Tree
Yellow Wood
Amur Maakia
Chinese Chestnut
Eastern Redbud.
American Beech
European Fern Leaf Beech
Weeping European Beech

Purple European Beech
White Oak
Swamp white Oak
Shingle Oak
Pin Oak
Northern Red Oak
Black Oak
Ginko
Large Fothergilla
Ohio Buckeye
Bottlebrush Buckeye
Hypericum
Pignut Hickory
Western Hemlock
Glossy Buckthorn
Serviceberry
Holmes Hawthorn
Gold Flame Spirea
Purple Plum
Skip Laurel
Otto Lucken Skip Laurel
Weeping Cherry
Japanese Skimmia
Japanese maple
Tamukeyama Japanese Maple
Norway Maple
Red Maple
Sugar Maple
Virginia Sweetspire
Tree of Heaven
Carolina Silverbell
English Yew
Washington English Yew

Tree of Heaven
Carolina Silverbell
English Yew
Washington English Yew
Japanese Yew
Chinese Elm
Japanese Zelcova

This recent inventory of trees at Florham indicates the range and variety that continues the Olmsted firm heritage and makes the landscape such a visual treat.

**Weeping Canadian Hemlock and
Pendant Silver Linden**

White Oak

Sugar Maple

American Holly

Crimson King Norway Maple

Black Oak

American Linden

Nordmann Fir

70

Red Oak

Shingle
Oak

Japanese Scholar Tree

London
Plane
Tree

White Pine

Blue Atlas Cedar

This Davey Tree Surgeons advertisement from the May 1918 issue of *House and Garden* notes that prominent clients include Mrs. H. McKay Twombly and Mrs. W. A. M. Burden, who was Mrs. Twombly's daughter. One hundred years later, the Davey firm maintains the grounds of the Florham campus.

The same *House and Garden* issue includes a testimonal for O.K. Plant Spray by Mrs. Twomby's superintendent, R. E. Tyson.

FLORHAM FARMS

As Hamilton Twombly from 1890 through the first half of 1893 was debating with his architects and landscape architect whether to upgrade and enlarge the Danforth estate along Madison Avenue or build a new mansion farther into his acreage on the other side of the railroad tracks that bisected his property, work began in earnest in 1890 on developing a farm on the back 900 acres of the 1,200 acres he had cobbled together through the purchase of thirty-seven parcels. So important was the farm to Twombly's conception of his country estate that the family often called this estate "The Farm." Twombly's daughter Ruth once noted that it was her father's dream that his only son Hamilton, Jr., "would love the Farm as much as he did."

Evidence of Twombly's early commitment to the Farm was McKim, Mead and White designing the farm complex with barns (the main barn was 250 feet long by 90 feet wide, with a height of 60 feet), stables that could hold 100 horses, a blacksmith shop, a wagon shop and two staff houses built in a square around a center circle. This area would be surrounded by vegetable gardens, orchards and fields for crops. A large clock atop a water tower was situated in the center of the circle.

Hamilton Twombly's model farm was his hobby, his passion and his challenge. He ran it on the most current scientific principles, just as George Vanderbilt was doing on his Biltmore estate in Asheville, North Carolina, and, being the consummate businessman, Twombly ran the Farm as a business enterprise. It was one of the few gentleman farms of that era that was run profitably.

"Millionaires as Farmers," an article in a 1899 issue of *The Conservative*, offered the characteristics of wealthy farmers like Hamilton Twombly: "… his grounds are the most expensive that money can buy; his barns are princely structures; his hot-house plants are the finest that soil and science can produce; his milk is skimmed and churned by the latest methods; his cow is nurtured as kindly as a baby. She is guarded by day and by night; her food must be of the most delicate flavor; the water she drinks must be flavored; she had mats to lie on and her horns are polished."

At the Farm's peak, it included 160 Guernsey cattle, 24 of which won prizes at the St. Louis World's Fair in 1904 and brought Mr. Twombly recognition as the premier Guernsey breeder in the United States. There were 400 cows (including one which in 1905 produced 790 pounds of butter in a year), that produced annually over one million gallons of milk, which, when sold in the neighboring towns from a wagon drawn by a pair of Thoroughbreds in gold mounted harnesses, netted $40,000 a year. One hundred South Down sheep tended by shepherds helped keep the lawns trimmed. Flowers and vegetables grown on the estate produced another $25,000 each year and two day old calves were sold for as much as $2,000 each.

Of course, it was just the surplus of the bounty of Florham that was being sold. Chef Donon would request whatever he needed for the day's menu and it would be brought to his kitchen door at Florham, or transported to the Twomblys' home in New York City during the winter months. When the family was at Vinland, their home next to The Breakers in Newport, the order would be loaded onto a railroad car at the private siding at Florham, hauled to Hoboken, New Jersey, then shipped overnight by American Express to the Fall River Boat line, then taken by truck to Vinland to be there early in the morning. With all the ingredients from Florham, Chef Donon was able to satisfy Mrs. Twombly's one demand: to prepare "the best of the best."

This full-page advertisement that appeared in the May 1926 issue of *Country Life* includes the offering of "three outstanding daughters of Ultra Select," a son and grandson of Ne Plus Ultra and the sire of eleven daughters. J.L. Hope was the farm manager at the time.

The FLORHAM FARMS Consignment

to the Guernsey Sale at the Interstate Fair Grounds, Trenton, N. J.

Thursday, May 20th, 1926

under the management of the Herrick-Merryman Sales Company: 25 females, over half with A. R. records and a truly representative collection from the Florham herd which has been for many years the source of foundation seed stock for successful breeders.

ULTRA LIL, a daughter of Ultra Select. She is third in New Jersey Class G; 10,518.3 lbs. milk, 566.9 lbs. butter fat.

*

ULTRA TANG, another daughter of Ultra Select, second in New Jersey Class G; 11,788.3 lbs. milk, 607.34 lbs. butter fat.

FLORHAM SELNORA, A.R. 17702; 11,839.0 lbs. milk, 566.7 lbs. fat, Class G. She is a daughter of Lone Pine Senator and her dam is a line bred Glenwood.

*

FLORHAM THEARA. This is another daughter of Lone Pine Senator now on test in Class G.

IMP. FRANCE'S JOY III. A line bred France cow now on A. R. test. One of the very good specimens of this famous family.

*

ROYAL MAID OF LINDA VISTA; 11,425.9 lbs. milk, 638.25 lbs. fat, Class A. She is a daughter of Don Filippo of Linda Vista, the sire of Maxim of Linda Vista, which sired the two ranking cows in Classes D and F.

The FLORHAM FARMS OFFERING

includes our three outstanding daughters of Ultra Select. Besides the two daughters pictured above we are including Florham Serene, 591.54 lbs. butter fat, Class E. Ultra Select, which is a son and grandson of Ne Plus Ultra, now has eleven daughters in the Advanced Registry, six of which average 654.51 lbs. fat in the young classes. The Florham Farms herd is Federal Accredited and our entire consignment will be sold subject to the agglutination blood test for infectious abortion. The sale will include a selection of about twenty head of the herd of Mr. R. L. Benson and a few top quality animals from other herds. Our offering may be inspected at any time previous to the sale at Madison, N. J., just a short distance from New York City on the Lackawanna Railroad.

THE WORKERS WHO BUILT AND MAINTAINED FLORHAM

At its peak, Florham employed more that one hundred men and women to maintain the farm and the grounds, service the equipment, drive the limousines, tend to the horses, prepare meals, and maintain the Mansion. The great majority remain anonymous beyond their names on index card records of work periods and wages. Fortunately, Friends of Florham newsletters acquired the stories of two of those workers—one there at the beginning and the other when the estate was a thriving operation.

An Immigrant from Italy

Representative of the workmen who constructed Florham and then settled in Madison was Salvatore Luciano, who came from Italy to New Jersey in the 1890s, just as Florham was being built. Like many of the other immigrants newly arrived in Hoboken, the then young Mr. Luciano was met at dockside by a labor contractor who signed him up for and transported him to his work on the Twomblys' estate then being created.

Mr. Luciano's first assignment, his descendants recall, was assisting his fellow immigrants in digging the trench for the footings of what was to become the mansion. Each day, the contractor deducted as a commission ten cents from Mr. Luciano's seventy-five-cents-a-day wage. To save up enough money to pay for his wife's trip from Italy to the U.S., the brand-new American citizen therefore had to take on a second after-hours job, cooling off horses for two hours each evening for local equestrians. After two years of this far from lucrative "double dipping," he had enough to cover his bride's trans-Atlantic fare and to begin his family in his new country.

A direct line to these early days of Florham and its workers like Mr. Luciano is his son, Pasquale, who turned 95 last April 24. Pat, as his family and friends know him, is something of a living source of local history. He recalls vividly the adversity faced by his parents and other working families of Madison in the late nineteenth and early twentieth centuries. Not a little of that adversity undoubtedly resulted from the perception longer-established residents had of their more recently arrived neighbors. Such a perception is unmistakably and distressingly revealed in a *Madison Eagle* article of April 21, 1911, reporting on the arrival of yet another group of newcomers:

"Fifty-five swarthy Italian laborers," the article began, "arrived in Madison Monday morning and have been industriously at work since on the lower end of Main Street, preparing to lay tracks for the Morris

County Traction Company ... The Italian laborers reached Madison at 7:48 o'clock from a New York city employment agency and an hour later were divided into squads and marched down Main street to Union avenue, where they were put to work with pick and shovel. ... The Italian workmen brought here for the job are an interesting lot. They attracted considerable attention Monday morning on the Green & Pierson lot adjoining the D., I., & W. tracks, where they were herded until taken to the scene of operations. They are all dark little fellows, the majority being small of stature but stockily built and fully capable of the hard physical labor they will be subjected to daily. ... Each Italian carried a bundle containing what little clothing he had brought with him. There were very few suitcases and no trunks. The most conspicuous were the large bundles with blankets or sheert for coverings, although all the belongings some had were contained inside a large colored handkerchief. The men will be quartered in the large shanty erected by Contractor Charles Ippolito on Burnet Road close to North Street for his sewer employees. It is said that between 300 and 400 Italians can be quartered in the large room this building affords for sleeping and living quarters all in one. Bunks are erected along the walls and here the men sleep, huddled together like so many cattle. ..."

Workers at leisure on the Florham farm

While Salvatore's son Pat recalls the severely challenging circumstances confronting his family in that era—his early boyhood home was a house lacking electricity, central heat, and an indoor toilet, and life in general was often difficult-he has also an endless supply of happy memories of his father's steady rise from Florham laborer to farmer and landowner. He can happily remember, also, his own successes as a grocery-store employee who became a food merchant and eventual owner of three Main Street buildings now housing at least eight businesses.

Some of his fondest recollections are of images of the Madison of long years ago, when the Twomblys' stately country home his father helped to build was in its brightest new days: children sledding undisturbed by traffic on what is now Maple Street, Main Street horse races on weekends, the YMCA located in the second floor of what is now a central Madison store, a gated street-level railway crossing in the center of town, a boggy morass where the Early Trades and Crafts Museum now is, the trolley that ran down Main Street and Park Avenue, and riding it with his wife more than six decades ago to see the premier presentation of *Gone With the Wind* at the newly opened Community Theater in Morristown.

Many of these recollections Pat views through the blue haze of the cigar smoke that is virtually a permanent wreath around his head as he sits on most fine days on a bench or chair out• side his Main Street apartment. He has smoked but never inhaled-five six-inch cigars a day since he was 15, he recently confessed. When told that, at that race, he has gone through approximately 9.8 miles of cigars, he laughed and said that he is going to have engraved on his tombstone the message that the cigars "kept the germs away."

The distance Pat Luciano's cigars would span if laid end to end is indeed considerable. But it is little more than a few small steps compared to the strides made by the workers who, like his father, helped build not only the Twomblys' magnificent home and estate but also the country chosen as a new homeland by the scores of people whom the Friends had gratefully in mind in restoring the Italian Gardens.

Adapted from the Friends of Florham newsletter Fall 2000

Builders of the Farm Structures, 1895

First row: Sam Gruver, Michael Tracey, Clinton Earley, Owen Rogers, Andrew Meehan, Val O'Neil, Jim Scaron, James Patterson, Joseph Bolon, Lawson Taylor. Second row: Art Long, Pat Dormady, John McKenley, Dave Conklin, Mike Flynn, Patrick O'Brien, Tommy Burns, Dan Babbit, Harold Hope (the little boy), James Brice, J. B. Hope.

This rare photograph depicts the group of men involved in building structures on the Florham Farm, a work in progress when they posed before the water tower in 1895. The farm had been functional for two years as additions were being made. This photograph was given to the *Madison Eagle* weekly by Patrick O' Brien, who had been the farm foreman for twenty years. It was printed on January 21, 1958.

Madison Mayor Jack Dunne's Memories

Years before he began his thirty-one years of service as a Detective-Patrolman in Madison, New Jersey, and later as a Deputy Chief of Detectives in the Morris County Prosecutor's Office and later mayor of Madison, "Jack" Dunne started his four-year career of after-school and summer-time "Florham" labors in 1947. That was the year in which Mrs. Twombly was seriously injured and permanently disabled in an auto accident in Newport. He therefore never saw the grande dame who for approximately five decades presided over "Florham" and its extravagant and elegant social events that were a celebrated distinction of one of the most acclaimed of America's greatest country homes.

Jack, however, often saw "Miss Ruth," as Ruth Twombly, the third of the Twomblys' four children was known among the estate's employees. "We weren't' really supposed to see her," he remembers. "One of the first instructions I got when I began work was not to look at Miss Ruth. We were supposed to turn our backs if she came into view."

He recalls a similar sort of prohibition about the behavior of workers entering the Mansion. "We were required to enter the building only through the service door at the rear. The one time I actually did enter the Mansion through the front door, the men I was with and I all stood stock still as soon as we stepped into the hallway, looking around wide-eyed." Half a century later, he still feels, he admits, some of that teenage awe, whenever he revisits the Great Hall of the Mansion.

His work related mostly to the grounds and greenhouses, as an assistant to painters and greenhouse and gardens workers. With the former, he painted the inside of the large green wooden fence that once ran around the perimeter of the estate. He joined the latter group in numbers of chores. At the approach of winter, they carried boxwood bushes and fig trees into the tree shed, where, he still recalls, he was tempted to violate a cardinal rule by sampling one of the nectarines ripening on the branches.

He participated in two special Saturday morning duties: helping to rake the gravel path running from the railway stop on which "Miss Ruth" would walk upon her weekend arrivals and assisting a gardener by bearing large numbers of potted plants from the greenhouses to the Playhouse swimming pool. There, they were arranged in 6-foot by 6-foot pyramidal banks for "Miss Ruth" to inspect and enjoy in the building created especially for her. The Playhouse area was the site of another of his randomly assigned tasks: spreading and patting down cotton seed on the surface of the putting green once located beside the building that was recently torn down and replaced by a new academic building.

The approach of the annual flower show in Madison Square Garden, Mayor Dunne also remembers, was a time of great activity for those responsible for the greenhouses and gardens. All members of the sizable crew began preparing for the show two months in advance by lavishing attention upon whatever plants might have been considered possible entries in that most prestigious contest. "For those two months, everything was aimed at the show," he said. On rainy days, the entire grounds crew repaired to the greenhouses to wash plant pots. Two women, he added, were regularly busy year-round in the greenhouses, tying up, potting, and trimming plants.

Some of his most vivid recollections of his "Florham" days are of the people with whom he worked. "'Florham' employees came to work wearing shirts and ties," he recalls, noting that the painters even kept their ties on at work, after having pulled overalls on over their clothes. To this day, he looks back fondly upon two of his immediate superiors, Basil Fillipone and Charles Massiello, responsible respectively for guiding the work of the greenhouse staff and overseeing the vegetable garden that once flourished where the Hamilton Park Executive Conference Center now stands.

His experiences at "Florham" have left the Mayor with a still-strong regard for a place that provided him with his very first gainful employment. "I remember one day in particular," he recently told a listener. "I was walking to work as a kid. It was a fairly long walk that took me by the Dodge estate across from the Twomblys' property. As I walked along, I looked down and saw a $20 bill on the path. I felt like a millionaire on my way to work for once!" The small treasure he happened upon was the equivalent of more than a week's wages when he began his four years at "Florham at $3.00 per day. Those daily wages rose to $6.00 by the time he left in 1950 to serve in the Korean War, "But I didn't get the increase without some resistance," he is prone to say with a nostalgic nod of his head. "Mr. Tyson, my boss in the paint crew, responded to my request for a raise with a playfully sarcastic question intended as a put-down of me for my being short: 'Why? Can't you reach the top of the fence?'"

Two years after Mr. Dunne left, Mrs. Twombly was to die, in April of 1952. Two years after that, Ruth Twombly was also to die, as the result of a fall at the Ritz Hotel in Paris. In the next year occurred the storied auction that was to mark, officially, the departure of the Twomblys from the magnificent house and grounds that, like the town that abutted the estate's northern border, bore a title representing a blending of the first names of its two founders, Florence and Hamilton Twombly.

The "Florham" that Major Dunne and his fellow workers knew would live on only in memory

Adapted from the Friends of Florham newsletter Spring 2001

FLORHAM IN WINTER

A winter scene in 1936

FLORHAM ARBORETUM

AarbNet, The Interactive Community of Arboreta, accredited the Florham campus of Fairleigh Dickinson University as a Level I Arboretum in November 2017. Here is the ArbNet description:

The Florham Arboretum is situated on the Fairleigh Dickinson University campus in Madison, NJ. It is the former Florham estate of Florence Vanderbilt Twombly and Hamilton McKown Twombly developed in the 1890's. Some notable landscape architects who had a role in its landscape were: Frederick Law Olmsted, the Olmsted Brothers. Warren H. Manning and Brinley and Holbrook. Management of the estate's landscape and greenhouses was under the direction of Arthur Herrington, noted horticulturalist and plant breeder, who came to Florham from Kew Gardens, England.

The main entrance is flanked to the left by weeping European beech leading to an allee of American linden. Southern Japanese hemlock, Western hemlock, Washington English yew, and a grove of Japanese false cypress grace the approach to the Mansion. Adorning the great lawn in front of the Mansion are two large specimens of Cedar of Lebanon, a large Nordmann fir, a large weeping Canadian hemlock, and a spectacular linden (Tilia "Petiolaris'). They have a large collection of common boxwood greater than 15 feet in height and width. To the north west of the Mansion stand oaks that originated prior to the estate development that were plotted on the 1890 topographic site survey.

1 Pine Oak, 2 Black Oak, 3 Pignut Hickory, 4 Linden, 5 American Basswood, 6 American Holly, 7 Maple, 8 Shingle Oak, 9 White Oak, 10 Sweet Bush, 11 Shellbark Hickory, 12 Sugar Maple, 13 Liquidambar, 14 Black Walnut, 15 Ginko, 16 Sugar Maple, 17 Chestnut

Congratulations to Fairleigh Dickinson University, Florham for earning 2017 Tree Campus USA® recognition. Tree Campus USA, an Arbor Day Foundation program, is celebrating its 10th anniversary. The Tree Campus USA program honors colleges and universities and their leaders for promoting healthy trees and engaging students and staff in the spirit of conservation.

To obtain this distinction, Fairleigh Dickinson University, Florham has met the five core standards for sustainable campus forestry required by Tree Campus USA, including establishment of a tree advisory committee, evidence of a campus tree-care plan, dedicated annual expenditures for its campus tree program, an Arbor Day observance and the sponsorship of student service-learning projects. Your entire campus community should be proud of this sustained commitment to environmental stewardship.

If ever there was a time for trees, now is that time. Communities worldwide are facing issues with air quality, water resources, personal health and well-being, and energy use. Fairleigh Dickinson University, Florham is stepping up to do its part. As a result of your commitment to effective urban forest management, you are helping to provide a solution to these global challenges.

SOURCES

Books

Albrecht, Donald and Jeannine Falino, editors. *Gilded New York: Design, Fashion, and Society.* Museum of the City of New York, The Monacelli Press, 2013.

Bere, Carol, Samuel Convissor, Walter Cummins, Mark Hillringhouse, Arthur T. Vanderbilt II *Florham: An American Treasure.* Madison, NJ: The Friends of Florham, Fairleigh Dickinson University, 2016.

Bere, Carol, Samuel Convissor, and Walter Cummins. *Florham: The Lives of an American Estate.* Madison, NJ: The Friends of Florham, Fairleigh Dickinson University, 2011.

Beveridge, Charles E. and Rocheleau, Paul. *Frederick Law Olmsted: Designing the American Landscape.* New York: Rizzoli, 1998.

Broderick, Mosette. *Triumvirate: McKim, Mead & White: Art, Architecture, Scandal and Class in America's Gilded Age.* New York: Knopf, 2010.

Burden, Shirley. *The Vanderbilts in My Life.* New York: Ticknor & Fields, 1981.

Burden, Wendy. *Dead End Gene Pool.* New York: Gotham Books, 2010.

Burden, William A.M. *Peggy and I: A Life too Busy for a Dull Moment.* New York: W.A. Burden, 1982; second printing, 1983.

Cavanaugh, Cam. *In Lights and Shadows: Morristown in Three Centuries.* Morristown: Morristown Library, 1986.

Cummins, Walter, Arthur T. Vanderbilt II. *"The Richest and Most Famous, Private Chef in the World": Joseph Donon: Gilded Age Dining at Florham with Florence Vanderbilt Twombly.* Madison, N.J., Florham Books, 2017..

Donon, Joseph. *The Classic French Cuisine.* New York: Alfred A. Knopf, 1937.

Foreman, John, and Robbie Pierce Stimson. *The Vanderbilt and the Gilded Age: Architectural Aspirations*, 1879-1901, New York: St. Martin's Press, 1991.

Kaschewski, Marjorie: *The Quiet Millionaires: The Morris County That Was.* Morristown, N.J. Daily Record, 1982.

King, Robert B. *The Vanderbilt Homes.* New York: Rizzoli, 1989.

Martin, Justin. *Genius of Place: The Life of Frederick Law Olmsted.* Cambridge, MA: DaCapo Press, 2011.

Patterson, Jerry. *The Vanderbilts.* New York: Harry N. Abrams, 1989.

Pratt, Lois, ed. *Samuel A. Pratt: The First Decade of Campus Development.* Madison, NJ: Fairleigh Dickinson University, 1999.

Rae, John W. *Mansions of Morris County.* Images of America series. Charleston, SC: Arcadia Publishing, 1999.

Rae, John, and John Rae, Jr. *Morristown's Forgotten Past – "The Gilded Age".* Morristown, NJ: John W. Rae, 1979.

Roper, Laura Wood. *FLO: A Biography of Frederick Law Olmsted.* Baltimore & Lond: The Johns Hopkins University Press, 1973; 1983.

Sammartino, Peter. *I Dreamed a College.* South Brunswick and New York: A.S. Barnes and Company, 1977.

Vanderbilt, Arthur T. *Fortune's Children: The Fall of the House of Vanderbilt.* New York: Morrow, 1989.

White, Samuel G. and Elizabeth White. *The House of McKim, Mead & White.* New York: Rizzoli, 1998.

…. *Stanford White, Architect*, New York: Rizzoli,, 2008.

Williams, Joan M. *Morristown.* Images of America Series. Charleston, SC: Arcadia Publishing, 1996.

Manuscript Collections

Monninger Center, FDU Florham Campus: Archives from Burden Collection, and other materials related to family, house, other buildings, landscape and local history.

Morristown & Morris Township Library: Local History Collection

New York Historical Society: Site plans and structural drawings for various Vanderbilt mansions.

New York Public Library, Humanities and Social Sciences Division, Burden family papers and photographs.

Frederick Law Olmsted Archives, Brookline, Massachusetts.

Films

The Vanderbilt-Twombly Florham Estate: Filmed by Joseph Donon in 1934.
Script by Carol Bere, Samuel Convissor, Walter Cummins, Arthur T. Vanderbilt II: Narration by Professor Gary H. Darden. Friends of Florham, 2016.

"Treasures of New Jersey: Fairleigh Dickinson University Florham". NJ TV, 2017.

Other

Fairleigh Dickinson University Digital Archives: http://http://cdm16322.contentdm.oclc.org. Source for photos of house, landscape, and other buildings; and finding aid for archives.

Friends of Florham website: fdu.edu/fof and https://www.facebook.com/fdufriendsofflorham

The Twomblys of Florham; The Beginning and End of an Era. A conversation with Walter T. Savage, FDU emeritus professor of English, and Arthur T. Vanderbilt II, moderated by Carol Bere. March 29, 2009; http://view2.fdu.edu/fdu-in-motion/the-twomblys-of-florham/

ABOUT THE AUTHORS

Walter Cummins began teaching on the Florham campus in 1965. Now an emeritus professor of English, he is on the faculty of the MFA in creative writing and the MA in creative writing and literature. In addition to being the co-author of three previous books about Florham, he has published seven short story collections and a collection of essays and reviews titled *Knowing Writers*.

Linda Snyder is well acquainted with the Florham Fairleigh Dickinson University Florham campus as an alumna, Regional Center Learning Specialist, and Arboretum Committee member. Outdoor interests include photography, botany, native plants, and historic garden restoration.

Arthur T. Vanderbilt II, a graduate of Wesleyan University and the University of Virginia School of Law, is the author of many books of history, biography, memoirs and essays. He became fascinated with Florham while researching and writing his book *Fortune's Children: The Fall of the House of Vanderbilt*, now being made into a television series by HBO. He is an Honorary Trustee of the Friends of Florham and has written many articles for the Friends of Florham publication. He wrote an introduction for *Florham: The Lives of an American Estate*, and is one of the authors of *Florham: An American Treasure*, and of *"The Richest and Most Famous Private Chef in the World": Joseph Donon*. He appeared in the New Jersey TV documentary about Florham in its "Treasures of New Jersey" series.

Edward Zimmermann has been in the landscape industry for thirty-eight years, including eighteen years with The Davey Tree Expert Co. He studied forestry and business at Paul Smiths College and golf course and athletic field management at Rutgers University. He has managed landscapes and implemented garden designs for residential and commercial sites and for public schools. As Branch Manager for Davey at Fairleigh Dickinson University, he has conducted extensive research on the history of the Florham landscape and assisted the Florham Campus in becoming a Level 1 arboretum in 2017 and Tree Campus in 2018.

CPSIA information can be obtained at www.ICGtesting.com
Printed in the USA
BVIW12n1750170418
513350BV00002B/2